All About Skills

Concepts

by
Marilynn G. Barr

Publisher: Roberta Suid
Production: Little Acorn & Associates, Inc.

Entire contents copyright © 2002
by Monday Morning Books, Inc.

For a complete catalog, write to the address below:
Monday Morning Books, Inc.
PO Box 1134
Inverness, CA 94937

Call our toll-free number: 1-800-255-6049
E-mail us at: MMBooks@aol.com
Visit our Web site:
http://www.mondaymorningbooks.com

ISBN 1-57612-164-X

Printed in the United States of America
9 8 7 6 5 4 3 2 1

Contents

Introduction

Reinforce concepts such as up and down, over and under, left and right, big and little, full and empty, hot and cold with the activity sheets, game board, concept cards, and take-home books in this book.

Activity Sheets
Provide crayons, scissors, and glue for children to complete activity sheets.

Take-home Books
Make construction paper folders for children to make take-home books. Provide each child with one of the book covers (pages 5, 16, 27, 38) to color, cut out, and paste to the front of his or her folder. Write each child's name on the cover. Reproduce, cut off the tops of accompanying activity sheets, and staple inside folders for take-home skills practice books.

Concepts Concentration
Reproduce, color, laminate, and cut apart the concept cards on pages 60-64. Teach children how to play a game of "Concepts Concentration" with two to four players. Shuffle and place the cards face down on a playing surface. In turn, each player turns over two cards. If the cards match, the player keeps the cards and continues to play. If the cards do not match, the cards remain in the same position and are turned over. Then the next player takes his or her turn. Play continues until the cards are gone. The player with the most cards wins.

Which Way? Game Board
Make a concepts game board (pages 57-59) for children to practice the concepts of left, right, up, and down. Reproduce, color, cut out, and glue the game board patterns to the inside of a manila folder. Reproduce, color, cut out, and glue the spinner to a sheet of oak tag. Color and cut out the frogs or provide playing pieces for two to three players. In turn, each player spins and moves his or her marker, on the arrow path, the number of spaces shown on the spinner. When it's the same player's turn again, he or she must move in the direction of the arrow on the space (up, down, left, or right). The first player to "The End," wins.

Building With Concept Cards
Prepare a work station with a variety of craft supplies including small blocks, paper scraps, craft sticks, pom poms, glue, scissors, buttons, and straws. Provide each child with a corrugated cardboard base. Then have children build tabletop sculptures. Give them oral instructions as you turn over a deck with the following concept cards: up, down, over, under, left, right, in front, and in back.

I Can Color
Concepts.

Name

I Can Color Up and Down.

Color the apple **up** in the tree red.
Color the turtle **down** on the ground green.
Color the rest of the picture.

I can color **up** and **down**.

I Can Color Over and Under.

Color the airplane **over** the cloud blue.
Color the bird **under** the cloud red.
Color the rest of the picture.

I can color **over** and **under**.

I Can Color Left and Right.

The duck on the **left** is wearing a hat.
The duck on the **right** is wearing a bow.
Color the duck on the **left** orange.
Color the duck on the **right** yellow.

I can color **left** and **right**.

I Can Color Big and Little.

Color the **big** star on the flag yellow.
Color the **little** star on the ball green.
Color the rest of the picture.

I can color **big** and **little**.

I Can Color Full and Empty.

Color the **full** jar orange.
Color the **empty** jar yellow.

I can color **full** and **empty**.

I Can Color Soft and Hard.

The butterfly is on a **soft** pillow.
The turtle is on a **hard** brick.
Color the **soft** pillow pink.
Color the **hard** brick red.

I can color **soft** and **hard**.

I Can Color Old and New.

The **new** hat has a flower on it.
The **old** hat does not have a flower on it.
Color the **new** hat purple.
Color the **old** hat brown.

I can color **old** and **new**.

I Can Color Hot and Cold.

The cup has **hot** cocoa in it.
The glass has **cold** ice in it.
Color the **hot** cup brown.
Color the **cold** glass yellow.

I can color **hot** and **cold**.

I Can Color In Front and In Back.

The bear is standing **in front** of the fence.
The tree is **in back** of the fence.
Color the bear brown.
Color the tree green.

I can color **in front** and **in back**.

I Can Color Wet and Dry.

The duck in the pool is **wet**.
The duck under the umbrella is **dry**.
Color the **wet** duck orange.
Color the **dry** duck yellow.

I can color **wet** and **dry**.

I Can Cut and Paste
Concepts.

Name

I Can Cut and Paste Up and Down.

Cut out the apples. Paste one apple **up** in the tree. Paste one apple **down** on the ground.

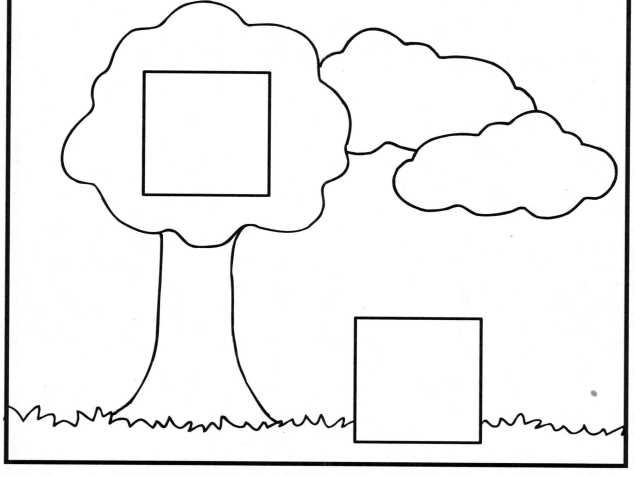

I Can Cut and Paste
Over and Under.

Cut out the airplane and the ship. Paste the airplane **over** the bridge. Paste the ship **under** the bridge.

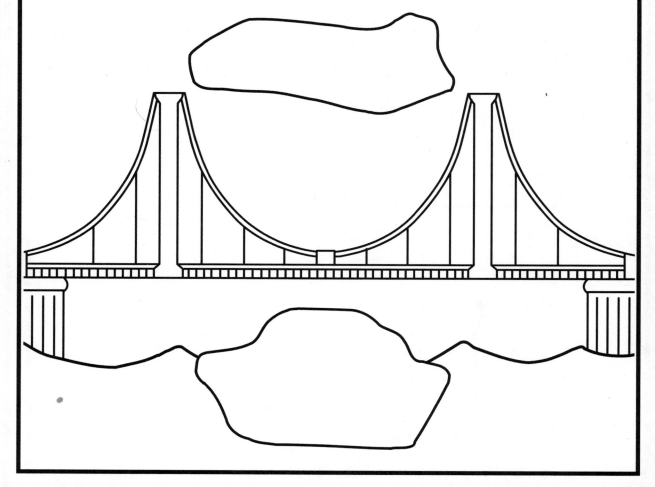

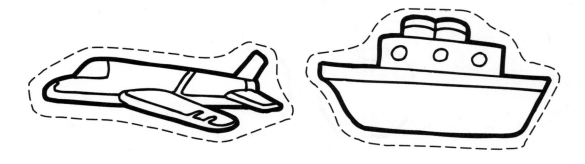

I Can Cut and Paste
Left and Right.

Cut out the doll and the bear. Paste the doll on the black stool on the **left**. Paste the bear on the white stool on the **right**.

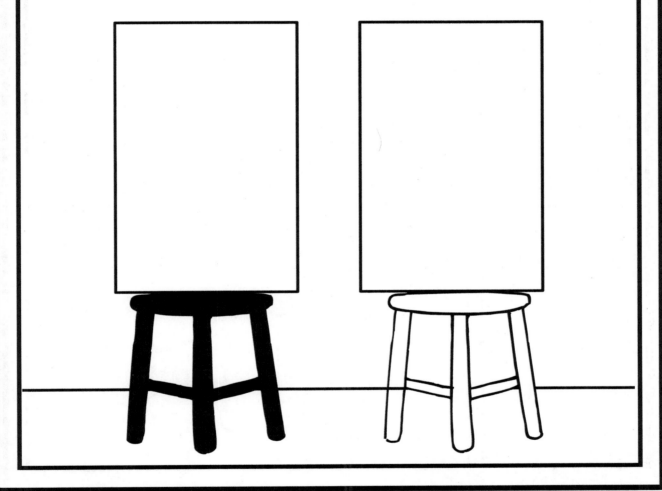

I Can Cut and Paste
Big and Little.

Cut out the stars. Paste the **big** star on the flag.
Paste the **little** stars in the sky.

I Can Cut and Paste Full and Empty.

Cut out the jars. Paste the **full** jar on the bear wearing a bow. Paste the **empty** jar on the bear without a bow.

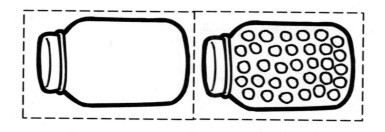

I Can Cut and Paste
Soft and Hard.

Cut out the bricks and the pillow. Paste the **soft** pillow on the chair. Paste the **hard** bricks on the fireplace.

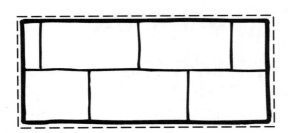

I Can Cut and Paste Old and New.

Cut out the hats. Paste the **old** hat on the doll wearing pants. Paste the **new** hat on the doll wearing a dress.

I Can Cut and Paste Hot and Cold.

Cut out the glass and pot. Paste the **hot** pot on the stove. Paste the **cold** glass on the refrigerator.

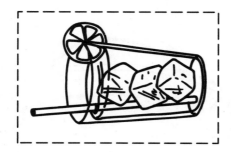

I Can Cut and Paste
In Front and In Back.

Cut out the fence and the bear. Paste the fence **in front** of the tree. Paste the bear **in front** of the fence. The fence is **in back** of the bear.

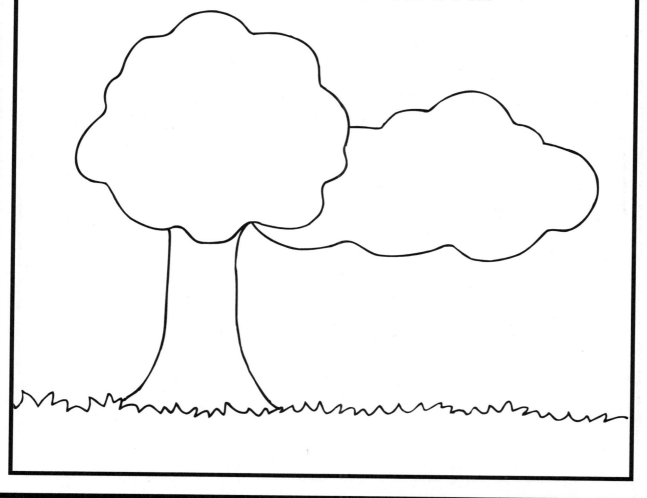

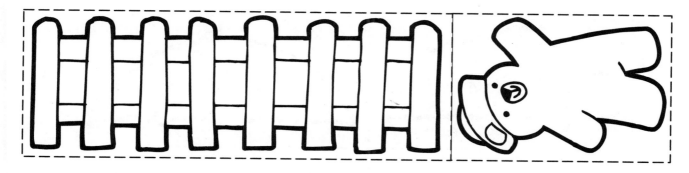

I Can Cut and Paste
Wet and Dry.

Cut out the cloud and the umbrella. Paste the cloud over the **wet** duck. Paste the umbrella over the **dry** turtle.

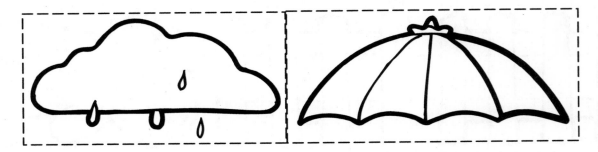

I Can Draw
Concepts.

_____

Name

I Can Draw Up and Down.

Draw an apple **up** in the tree.
Draw an apple **down** in the basket.
Color the picture.

I can draw **up** and **down**.

I Can Draw Over and Under.

Draw a cloud **over** the rainbow.
Draw a house **under** the rainbow.
Color the picture.

I can draw **over** and **under**.

I Can Draw Left and Right.

Draw red marbles in the bag on the **left**.
Draw black jelly beans in the jar on the **right**.
Color the picture.

I can draw **left** and **right**.

I Can Draw Big and Little.

Draw a **big** star on the flag.
Draw **little** stars around the flag.
Color the picture.

I can draw **big** and **little**.

I Can Draw Full and Empty.

Draw a jar **full** of beans on the black stool.
Draw an **empty** jar on the white stool.
Color the picture.

I can draw **full** and **empty**.

I Can Draw Soft and Hard.

Draw a **soft** pillow in the chair.
Draw **hard** bricks on the fireplace.
Color the picture.

I can draw **soft** and **hard**.

I Can Draw Old and New.

Draw an **old** hat on the standing bear.
Draw a **new** hat on the sitting bear.
Color the picture.

I can draw **old** and **new**.

I Can Draw Hot and Cold.

Draw a cup of **hot** chocolate for the bear wearing a scarf. Draw a glass of **cold** water for the bear wearing sunglasses. Color the picture.

I can draw **hot** and **cold**.

I Can Draw In Front and In back.

Draw a fence **in front** of the tree.
Draw the sun **in back** of the mountains.
Color the picture.

I can draw **in front** and **in back**.

I Can Draw Wet and Dry.

Draw rain and **wet** puddles on the ground.
Draw an umbrella to keep the duck **dry**.
Color the picture.

I can draw **wet** and **dry**.

I Can Color
Same and Different.

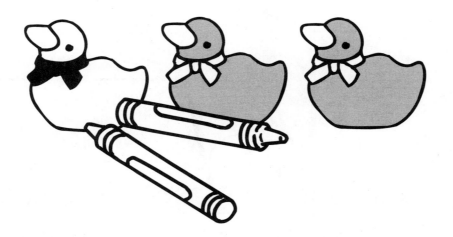

_____

Name

I Can Color Same Bears.

Look at the bears in each row.
Color the bears that are the **same** in each row.

I can color **same** bears.

I Can Color Different Turtles.

Look at the turtles in each row.
Color the turtles that are **different** in each row.

I can color **different** turtles.

I Can Color Same Rabbits.

Look at the rabbits in each row.
Color the rabbits that are the **same** in each row.

I can color **same** rabbits.

I Can Color Different Stars.

Look at the stars in each row.
Color the stars that are **different** in each row.

I can color **different** stars.

I Can Color Same Ducks.

Look at the ducks in each row.
Color the ducks that are the **same** in each row.

I can color **same** ducks.

I Can Color Different Flowers.

Look at the flowers in each row.
Color the flowers that are **different** in each row.

I can color **different** flowers.

I Can Cut and Paste Same and Different.

Name

I Can Cut and Paste
Same Hearts.

Look at the hearts in each row.
Cut out and paste the heart that is the **same** in each row.

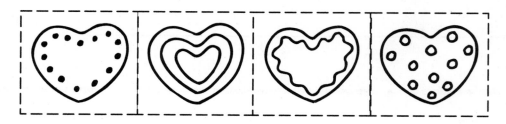

I Can Cut and Paste Different Bears.

Look at the bears in each row.
Cut out and paste a **different** bear in each row.

I Can Cut and Paste
Same Ducks.

Look at the ducks in each row.
Cut out and paste the duck that is the **same** in each row.

I Can Cut and Paste Different Stars.

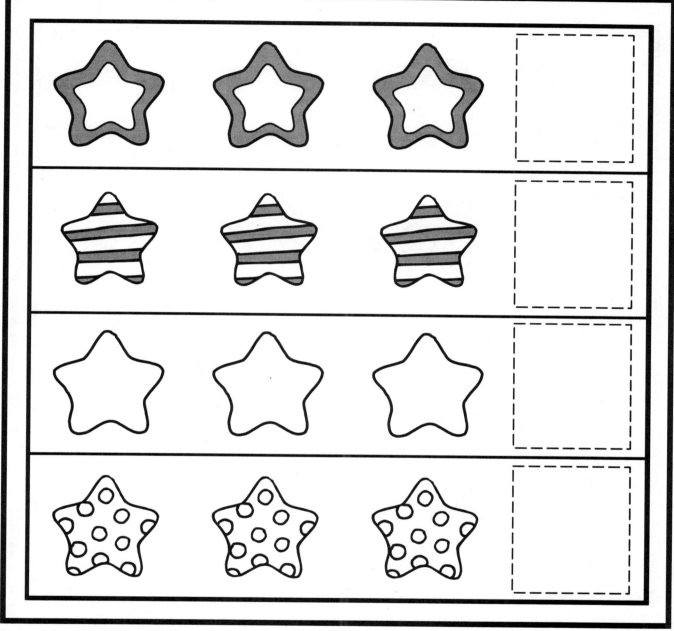

Look at the stars in each row.
Cut out and paste a **different** star in each row.

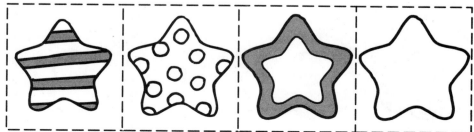

I Can Cut and Paste
Same Flowers.

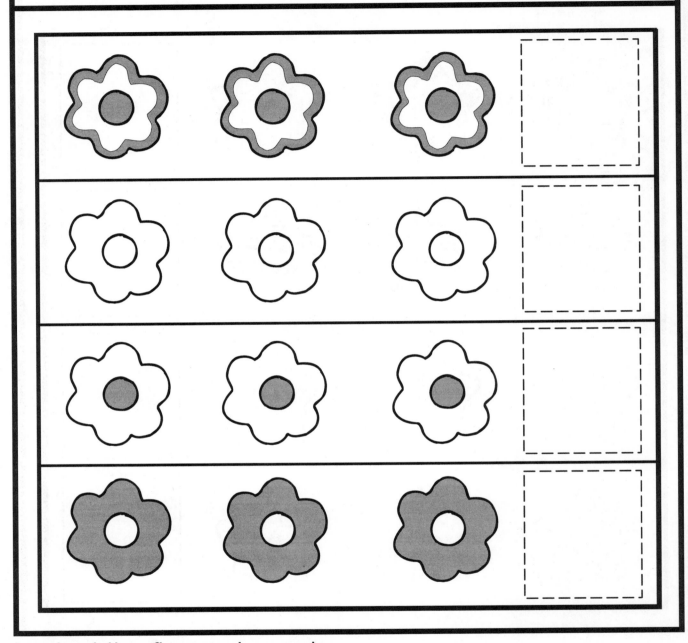

Look at the flowers in each row.
Cut out and paste the flower that is the **same** in each row.

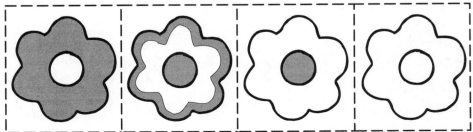

I Can Cut and Paste Different Rabbits.

Look at the rabbits in each row.
Cut out and paste a **different** rabbit in each row.

I Can Cut and Paste
Same Things.

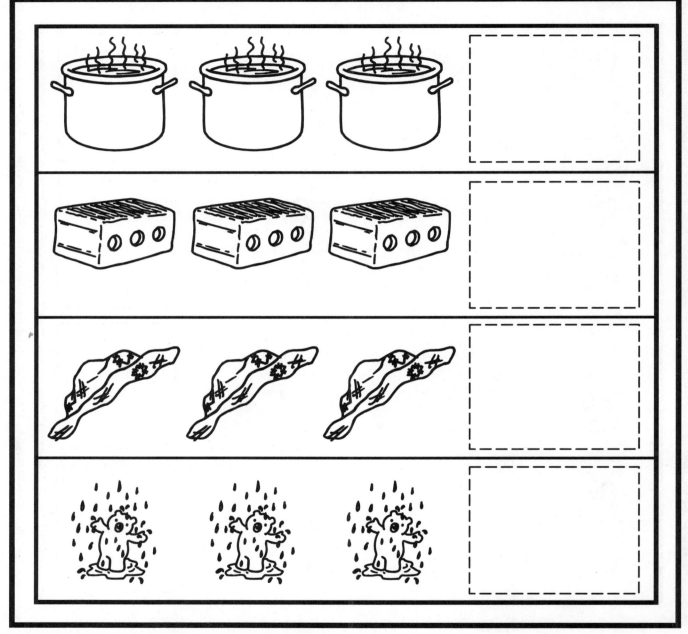

Look at the things in each row.
Cut out and paste the **same** thing in each row.

I Can Cut and Paste
Same Things.

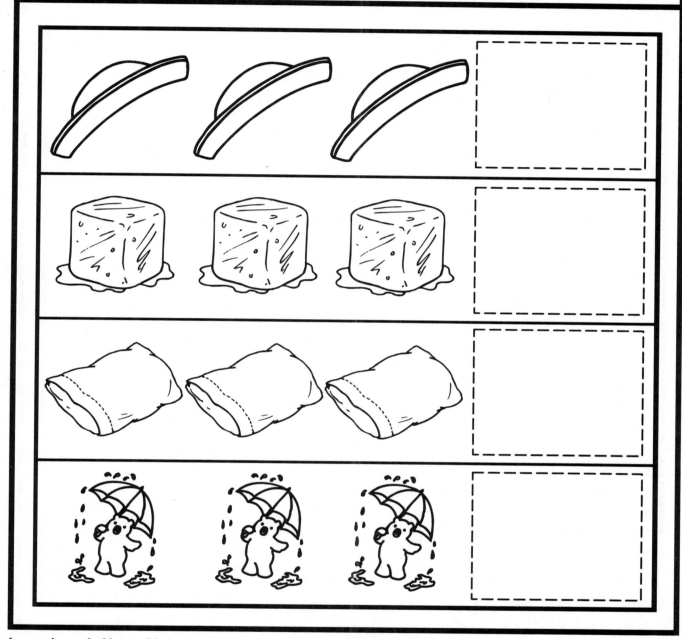

Look at the things in each row.
Cut out and paste the **same** thing in each row.

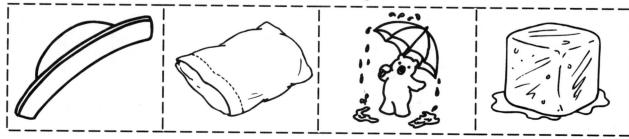

I Can Cut and Paste Same Arrows.

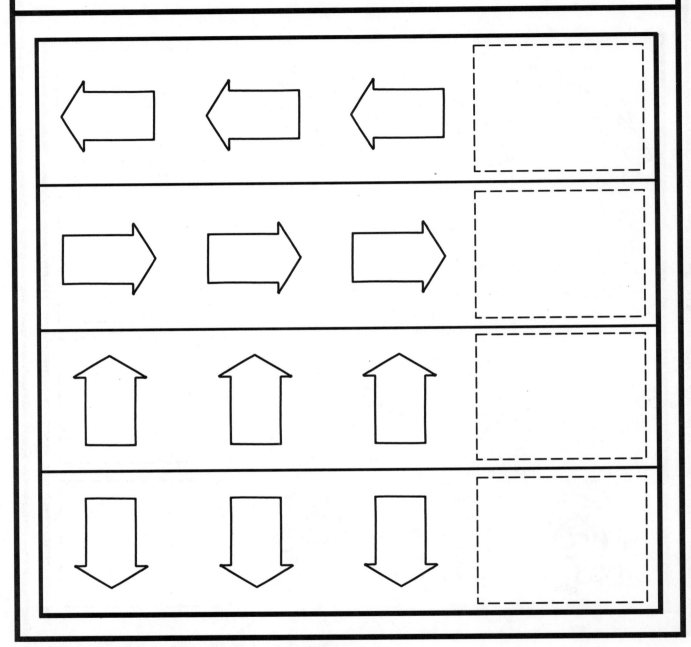

Look at the arrows in each row.
Cut out and paste the **same** arrow in each row.

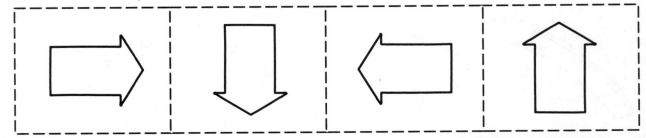

I Can Cut and Paste
Different Things.

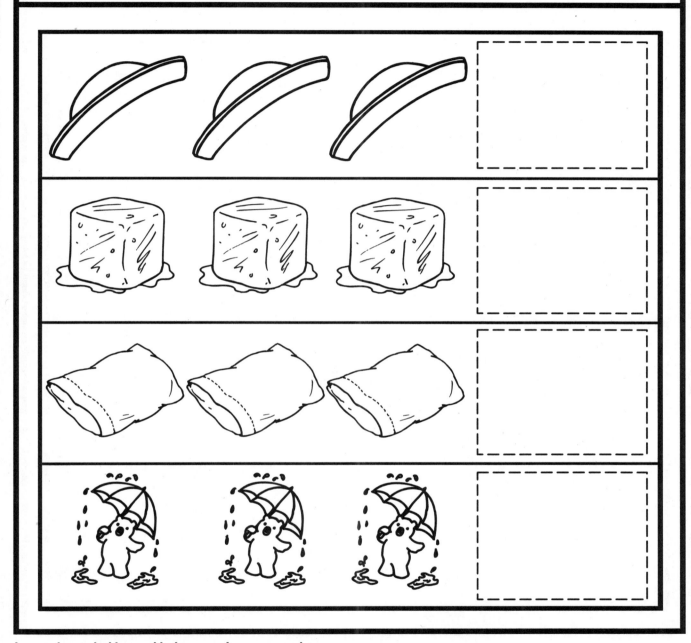

Look at the things in each row.

Cut out and paste a **different** thing in each row.

I Can Cut and Paste Different Arrows.

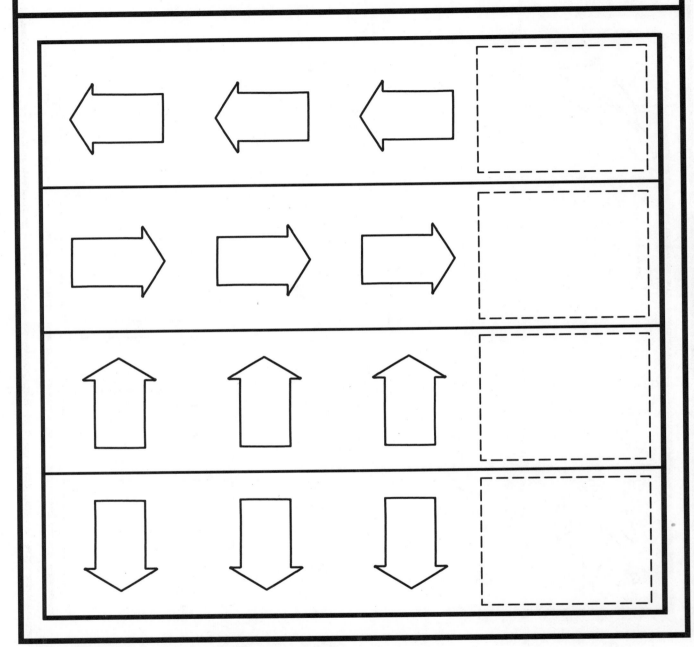

Look at the arrows in each row.
Cut out and paste a **different** arrow in each row.

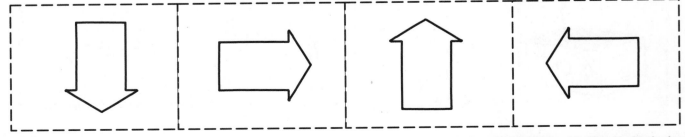

Which Way? Game Board

Which Way? Game Board

→	→	→	↓
↑			↓
←	↑		↓
	↑		↓
→	↑		↓
↑			THE END

Which Way? Spinner and Frogs

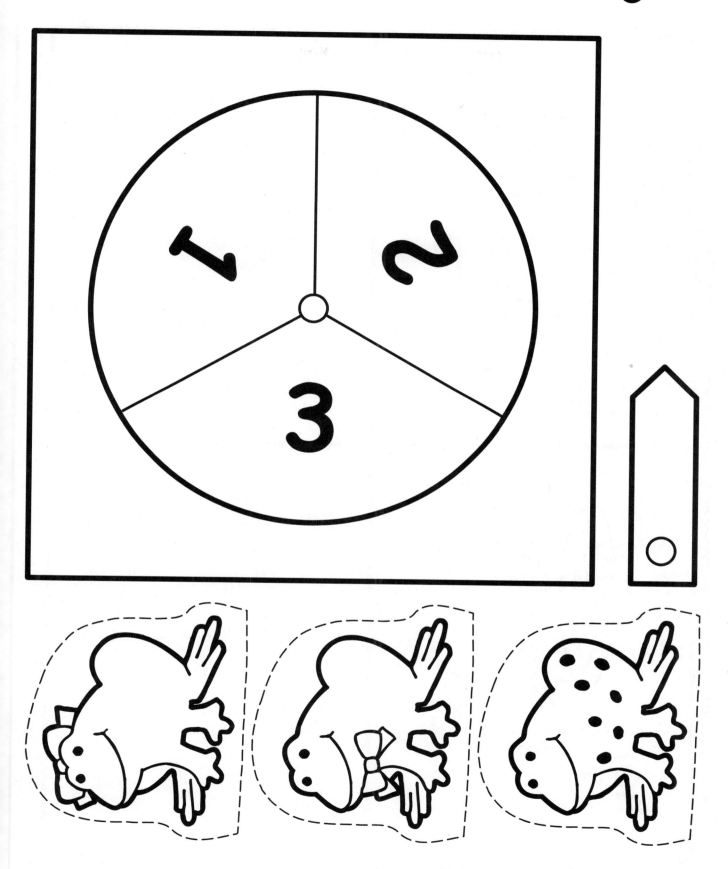

Concept Cards

cold

soft

hot

hard

Concept Cards

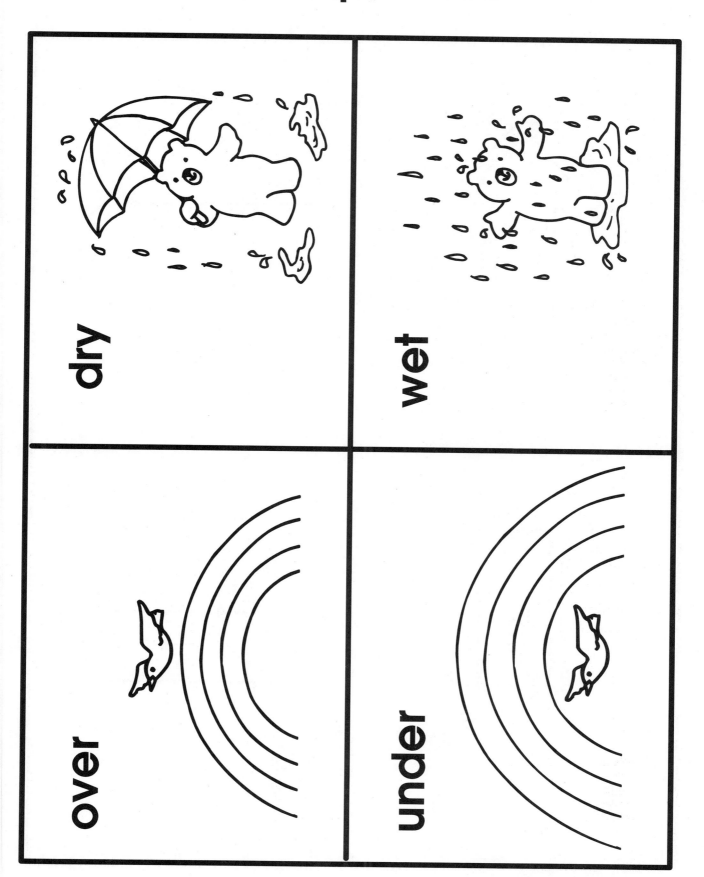

dry

wet

over

under

Concept Cards

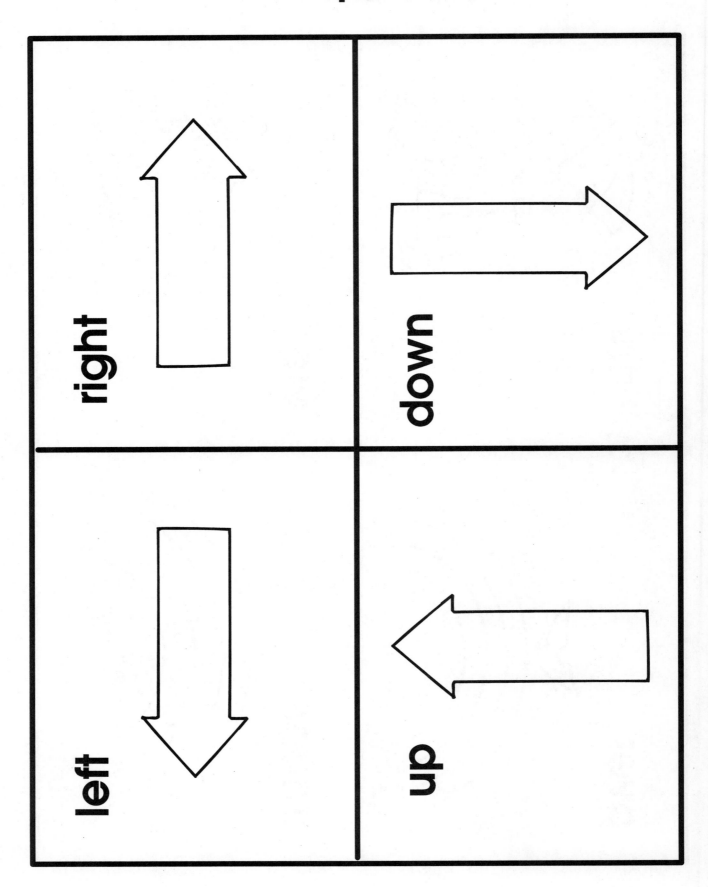

right

down

left

up

Concept Cards

little

empty

big

full

Concept Cards

in front

in back